MIND CONTROL

EVERYTHING YOU KNOW IS WRONG!

How Government Brainwashing Works

by Maurice Suraz

Table Of Content

Introduction

Welcome! First of all, thank you and congratulations for downloading this book *"Everything You Know Is Wrong- How Government Brainwashing Works"* I really appreciate you putting your time and trust in me. I am truly convinced that this book is able to provide you with the value and information you are looking for.

Since the dawn of sin and man, there has been a quiet and underlying desire of the few to control the masses. Naturally, even simple-minded creatures resist outside control: pets fight tooth and nail against getting medicine just as readily as a US citizen would resist being arrested without just cause. While we are all animalistic and primitive in ways, a few select individuals figured out how to band together, tell big lies to the population at large, and justify vast sweeping surrender of freedoms under the guise of security: all while being exonerated of the same expectations that the masses must endure.

We call these slimy, two-faced jerks politicians, and, typically, we vote them into office with flags waving and cheers abounding. Politics is mind control. Simply put, without controlling others' thoughts and feelings, politics wouldn't even be a popularity contest. It would be lost. In reality, agendas on both political sides are chosen well ahead of any term in office and neither stance on any issue between the Democrats or Republicans is impressively novel or representative of the will or best interest of the people. At this point, it may be frustrating knowing that voting, campaigning, protesting and otherwise engaging in the political system as we know it is futile. Often the question is posed, "how do I know that I have no control? I feel in control..." Frankly, the answer is,

Everything You Know is Wrong.

Chapter 1- Mind Control- Possible?

From the beginning of recorded history and presumably much further back, controlling the will of others has been a core objective of those who seek power, and/or a claim on having their legend go down in history. From Christian and Judeo mythology concerning Satan tempting Eve while disguised as a serpent, it is obvious that swaying the will of others is seen as an evil. Key protagonist figures in all religions point towards tolerance, love, peace and truth. Antagonists like Satan in this case are the "black magic" users: they speak lovely deceptions in the form of soothing hisses then STRIKE!

Two puncture wounds later, and you're infected. You become a zombie to the will of another. It is no small coincidence that Luciferian rituals are performed by the Illuminati – the goal of the elite is to stay in power and to secure their seat of power for as long into the future as possible. By effectively controlling masses of millions to billions of people, operations can continue for the global elite with relative ease.

However, just like another classic form of subtle mind control, the Trojan Horse can be brought before these idolaters of power and greed. What once served as a gateway for Spartans to invade Troy will be a microcosm of the power usurpation soon to come. As is well known, the Trojan Horse, (a towering wooden sculpture of a horse, built by the Spartans to house and hide several of their best warriors) was presented at the gates of Troy, which were rumored to be impenetrable.

Being art philanthropists and culturally decadent people, the people of Troy as well as the government embraced the horse sculpture as a gift. They welcomed it into the walls of the city, thus allowing the special operations team of Spartans to kill gatekeepers on the inside and let their forces in without setting off city-wide alarms. Troy was sacked within one night, however, the rise of the People against their brainwashers will be a slow process at first. It will grow quicker as more people accept the truth about their circumstance, and their oppressors.

Today's power mongers are receptive to only one thing: power and money. What they did not expect, were for so many individuals out of the masses to "wake up": basically snapping out of their mind control, then achieving relative self-sustainability off of the grid and ultimately spreading the message of how to break free. The People's Trojan Horse is our own jealousy of the freedom that the elite enjoy. Being rich and powerful is a desire of most people, but freedom is important first and foremost. With the immediacy of communication in the internet age, people are coming together and realizing that their will and action does make a difference. By spreading the message of freedom and assuring the pursuit of happiness for all, relatively unknown figures become known. Next, they become crowd-funded. What once was the vision of one is now the reality of many. Regular people become famous actors, celebrities and even politicians. Now a collective of personal wealth is being pooled to oppose the system of control that exists. As this popular enactment of will grows, it sees the snowball effect: exponentially more oppressed and brainwashed individuals will break free of their chains and join in the fight against those central, few families responsible for funding both sides of wars dating back before the Revolutionary War, and, who are responsible for the deaths and impoverishment of billions over the years of their stealthy reign.

All families that traded the livelihoods of billions of strangers for their own personal gain will lose the control that they've had over the ages – provided that the truth circulates. Similarly to the murder of Caesar where Brutus and the council stabbed him to death at night, each person that realizes the controls that surround them and chooses to resist them is a pin prick among hundreds of millions of others that are puncturing the dreams of families like the Waltons, the Rockefellers, the Rothschilds, the Astors, the DuPonts, the Kochs and the Kennedys. When the masses can easily identify the types of controls that affect them, they can break free of them and change the course of history.

First, to understand the objectives of those that work to control others' minds, it is ideal to look towards other natural deceivers of the world. Take for instance, the Venus Fly Trap. This simple organism has developed predatory instinct so much so that it lures, traps and liquefies life that exists higher on the evolutionary chain than itself. Flies, bees, wasps, ants... anything that has protein that finds its way into the sweet smelling "leaves" of the Venus Fly Trap gets trapped within the "jaws" of this ancient predator and made into a meal. From this, it becomes obvious that mind control is <u>dangerous</u>. Any entity that would want to lure you, soothe you or otherwise reprogram your thinking is doing so for exclusively <u>their own</u> benefit. Second, we can learn from the fungus *Ophiocordyceps unilateralis* that mind control; LITERAL mind control, is possible.

This fungus luckily only infects ants , (thusfar, but who knows what Monsanto's military branch has planned for this information) and what it does to spread is practically a page out of survival horror. It senses when the right type of ant is nearby, then, as a fungus spore, it releases and clings to the ant's cuticle. Next, it hardens and spreads across the ant's exoskeleton. Now, the fungus builds immense pressure against the ant's exoskeleton, (about the pressure of air in a 747 airplane tire) and bursts into the host. Once it grows around the brain, the fungus does not attack and kill the host – it actually secretes compounds that <u>take possession of the host's motor functions</u> and begins staging the host for mass infection of other ants. All of this occurs through <u>literal</u>, <u>natural</u>, and <u>chemical</u> brain control; the fungus leads the host away from the colony and causes it to act erratically. As an ant colony does when this happens, other ants will go to drag this "lame duck" into an ant graveyard. Somehow knowing that the ant colony does this, the fungus directs the host to climb to a low hanging leaf or branch of some close shrubbery or tree, and then it makes the host bite down on the stem of the leaf or the bottom of the branch, dangling over a crowd of very confused "pallbearer" ants. At this point, the fungus kills the host by invading the brain. It then grows as a stalk out from the head of the deceased host and releases spores over the ants from the colony below that are working to collect the dead ant to put it in the graveyard. These ants become infected and the process repeats. Lessons from this mind controlling terror are simple to identify: first, literal mind control IS possible. Second, it doesn't take a smart personality or mind to be a predatory mind controller – all it takes is the right programming. If fungus can do it, it's not far off to imagine humans taking advantage of this phenomenon as well. Lastly, the ocean is home to several other professional "con-men" species that use deception as a kind of mind control to catch a meal.

Angler Fish have a long, fishing pole appendage jutting out from the front of their head with a bioluminescent sphere at the end of it. Being that they live in the Mariana Trench where hardly any light exists, other fish swim over to see what this strange source of light is – CHOMP! Angler Fish have nightmarishly long and spiny teeth that grab prey and pull victims into the Angler's throat and stomach. Defensively, the Puffer Fish is a prime example of a fish propaganda expert. Upon feeling threatened, the tiny fish will fill up with water and expand to three to five times its previous size. If this response does not scare off a predator, the Puffer Fish has the added benefit of being extremely poisonous. Predators that don't take the Puffer Fish warning to "Back OFF" wind up dead, and other, smarter predators, (that leave the Puffers alone), reproduce and produce little fish that will, ideally, leave the Puffer Fish alone as well. Finally, the Stone Fish is an extremely poisonous fish that disguises itself as a rock by being:

   A) *very flat, and*

   B) *very bumpy and sediment colored*

As this jerk of a fish settles in amid camouflaging sediment, any prey that happens over it will be bitten and quickly consumed. People who step on Stone Fish can quickly die, as it's among the most poisonous fish in the world. From this, we learn that just because the path ahead looks free from pitfalls and devious traps doesn't mean it actually IS safe.

Whether found on land in the form of something as ancient and simple-celled as a fungus or in the sea using deceptive bait and kill tactics developed over millions of years of evolution, creatures great and small utilize forms of mind control to advance themselves and assure the survival of their species. Human beings, especially those with the most power and money to lose, have developed in similar ways, only the height of their deception has affected billions of people through the course of history.

Chapter 2- Early Government Brainwashing

Considering the level of corrupt control over masses of people that the US has achieved, it is not ironic that the Greek democracy was the birthplace of the precursor to modern day lobbyist, swindler, shyster, con-men and "mind control" experts. In Greece, there was a class of professionals who were called the Sophists. These were men that were considered wise about the world. They were practiced in persuasion and both worldly current events and groundbreaking philosophy. Sophists were perceived as notoriously deceptive among the people, primarily because of their exuberant charges and fees to the families of rising noblemen and Statesmen for the services of grooming a new "open-minded and wise" leader. If these people could be compared to a group of people nowadays, the best comparison would be that they are mere Self Help Gurus. The Sophists were the Grecian version of personalities like Zig Ziglar, Jim Rohn and other such "motivational speakers". Those who charge everyday people thousands of hard earned dollars for a seminar that lasts two hours, where at the end, all that the crowd has learned is where to purchase the speaker's CD's, videos, and of course, the opportunity to partake in the speaker's next great event, all for the low, low cost of... <insert exuberant amount here>. As a result of the rise of such swindlers as an accepted and respected professional group in addition to other factors of corruption, propaganda began to rise within Greece, though not exactly in the form as we think of it when in context with Nazis or the US agenda.

In Greece, wealthy families were the central, driving force behind commissioning art, research and other great developments in culture. Specifically, the Athenians were adept at developing plays, art and handwritten books that only the affluent could afford. Because of this, the plays and commissioned art would often be loaded with the opinions of the wealthy benefactor financing the piece. Religion, politics and moral conduct were all conveyed through art. Different families funding different plays may have developed entirely different perspectives on issues like government and morality. Even in cases when political agendas weren't overtly expressed as a theme, they still could be identified through the message that the financing family wanted the artist to convey. Remarkably similar was the political skewering done by "warring" newspapers during and after the Revolutionary War. Only a few printing presses were available across the newly formed nation, so the Founding Fathers would utilize the platform of news publications to promote their specific views. Rather than the standardized, Associated Press releases that all news channels use now, newspapers would affiliate themselves on very partisan grounds with famous politicians, for money, (sound familiar?) This mimicked the way that art through playwriting, gladiator game staging and other forms of cultural representation propagandized opposing views between Greek nobility for the masses. When it comes to outright propagandizing lies, the Nazis may have been the best known through history, but they were not the first.

"If you tell a big lie, and tell it frequently enough, it will be believed." ~ Adolf Hitler. While this mentality wasn't novel when Hitler came to power, he certainly honed it towards the mind control machine that we currently experience in first world nations. Originally, the propagandizing of flat out lies can be first recorded in history through the gripes of a poet, writer, politician and soldier named Sir Walter Raleigh. In 1588, the Spanish Armada suffered a devastating loss in battle against the British off of the cost of the Azures. According to Sir Raleigh,

> "[It is] no marvel that the Spaniard should seek by false and slanderous pamphlets, advisoes, and letters, to cover their own loss to derogate from others their own honours, especially in this fight being performed far off."

In plain English, Sir Walter Raleigh identified and warned of the Spanish deception of the people concerning the false reporting of significant events in the nation's military affairs. Sir Walter Raleigh also said of Spain,

> "*in sundry languages, in print, great victories in words, which they pleaded to have obtained against this realm [England]; and spread the same in a most false sort over all parts of France, Italy and elsewhere.*"

Quite obviously, Sir Walter Raleigh was describing the sort of mass indoctrination and propaganda campaign as was seen during Nazi control of Europe, as well as the type of control that STILL exists today in places like North Korea. Even the US media is extremely slanted in favor of pursuing profit and maintaining the status quo. Luckily for residents of the States, private media is protected free speech. This has led to alternative and reliable news outlets that report instances of government abuse such as CopBlock. As recently as August 2014 with the shooting of Michael Brown in Ferguson, MO, we know that the US government is increasingly ruling its' own citizens through fear of a police state on a Federal and State level. Members of the Press were arrested, detained, and let go hours later with no record of the incident, according to the police, afterwards. Lois Lerner "losing" her hard drive... Obama having no knowledge of Benghazi... This list goes on, but, the general freedom of speech that the private Press is afforded in the US makes the US a closer model to the Athenian model of nobility financiers that sway public opinion through art and entertainment. When it comes to outright government-issued false propaganda, North Korea is taking a page out of Spain's old playbook.

Despite being relatively poor, underdeveloped and small in land mass, North Koreas regularly publishes vast and outrageous claims through their State run media outlets. Such claims have included uncanny acts of heroism by their leader Kim Jong Un, but also audacious lies such as being the most winningest country in the past Olympics. They were in fact, not the most winningest team by a long shot. This is a direct derivative of the old Spanish trick that Hitler popularized in Germany during his rise to power. Lies in frequency publicized widely can significantly affect the psyche of the individual minds that make up the population.

Chapter 3- Similarities Between Old And New Governments

Settling the matter of private access to public speech is the old adage, "Money is Speech". If you have enough money, you can broadcast your message from coast to coast and change minds on a national level. Further, "Speech is Power" is a good constant – money does not always generate the source of speech. Sometimes, as in our next usurpation of power, it is the voice of the People that is being heard, loud and clear.

For example, money could buy Spain and North Korea all of the speech in their respective countries. However, even in repressed police states like North Korea, fringe-thinkers and revolutionaries spread truth at the risk of their lives. As more people hear doubts about the "official story", the propaganda loses its' effectiveness and a new lie, often bigger than the previous one must be devised. What the North Korean government would call "extremists", are actually regular people like protesters of the Occupy Movements, the Missouri protests or any other protest against repression. As some are caught and persecuted by torture or death, more rise in their wake. This is because oppression leads to rejection and reform.

Differing in approach, the Athenians did not spread lies: they may have embellished their names or represented values unpopular either with the people or the government; however these agendas were masterfully embedded in sculpture, painting, handwritten books and theater. Speech is an art. Even duels to the death at the Coliseum were sometimes staged as historical battles – obviously meant to inspire national pride and fervor for battle, IE: support for the military. Today, we find powerful speech in well financed sitcoms, movies and theater.

When a message is well-received, regardless of whether it was heavily financed or just simply popular, it makes the source of that message powerful. The source is credible now for having a popular position. They also have the opportunity to stay in the public eye and sway opinions through their positive influence. All said, money can <u>always</u> buy speech and speech will <u>always</u> fuel power. That does not mean that purchased speech will convince the masses, mostly because of individual informants that buck the State's position. It also doesn't mean that abuse of power can't /won't ruin a good message, even if it were crowd-sourced through popular will. Absolute power corrupts absolutely.

Current Federal US laws are archaic when it comes to practicality for the People, yet somehow the tax code has seen thousands of additional pages over the years and the veteran's affairs has backlogs of millions of paper files of claims for soldiers around the country. Millions of dollars are spent on "mind ops" in the military and while Our Founding Fathers worked to end tyrannical persecution, We, the People find ourselves entrenched in fees, fines and red tape, all courtesy of our "loving" government. When we protest, we used to be met with water cannons. Now there are LRAD's that emit high frequency audio pitches that can cause eardrums to rupture. Where real bullets were fired at Kent State, rubber bullets were seen used on rioters in Missouri, (but let it be noted that missed shots do not discriminate between peaceful protesters from the violent ones). While the US affords freedom enough that private Press and private interests can coordinate resistance to power abuse and mind control, the USA is becoming a police State where Press members are arrested without charge or record and where the government has literally started labeling The People a "domestic threat".

There are many countries currently pitted in social upheaval and political unrest that could be examined for deception and attempts at buying, swaying or literally mind controlling their people. Mexico, Egypt, Syria,

Afghanistan, Iraq, Iran, Jordan, Israel, Sierra-Leone, Congo, Ukraine and Russia are just a few of the better known countries that have had revolutions and civil war in the past hundred years or more recently. There is without a doubt a change coming across the globe as a result of free thinking radicals.

Free thinkers must be armed with knowledge, and it is in that spirit that the following information is being shared. It has been too long that our governments have used us like sheep. It has been too long that we have tolerated being sheared. People united in love and peace will overcome the evil that has swept across the globe in an attempt to bring it under one flag, and then control the Earth entirely. Mass mind control is not just a theory; it is something that governments have been striving for in the back corner, basement laboratories for decades.

Whether it's fluoridated water, ELF broadcast and RFID chipping or any other "insane" conspiracy, the people of the world, not just the People of the US, are threatened when the elite aim to control the dealings of the entire planet. To oppose a seemingly "too big to fail" force, each individual must be armed with the knowledge of how government mind control works and how it has been performed in the past. Once this is understood, conceptualizations of future technology and the possibility that our government tracking is much more advanced than we thought already, (as scary as that is to think, considering the drones, the 30,000x magnification scopes, the Microbot recording devices that look like insects and a steady push to make the ordinary citizen a criminal for integration into the criminal justice system) will be hypothesized.

What you read may scare you. It may cause you to question your past. It may make you think twice about the next news broadcast you watch. If it does anything, it should give you an idea of what our government has been *recorded* as doing concerning controlling the minds of others. While this is a peek, you should assume at all times that the rabbit hole goes much, much further down.

Chapter 4- Real Mind Control Of the 20th And 21st Century

It's clear that mind control is dangerous and present both within nature and in the traits and personalities of some humans. It takes the lives of countless victims, and most are totally ignorant to their plight up until death. Through many years and across the span of the globe, efforts to actually possess the minds of enemies or entire populations have been being made by governments. This is not fiction or speculation: this is a fact. Following are some of the most prevalent ways that citizens are indoctrinated by their government. Some are seemingly innocent: High Schools that get funds for high levels of college acceptance within their school, for instance. This, surprisingly enough, is a form of mind control. Then there are the more obvious forms of mind control: CIA experiments, hypnosis, putting people in medication-based psychosis to be used as sleeper agents or merely to sedate the populous at large... these all are confirmed efforts in mind control that have dawned within our age, much to our sleepy indifference. Hopefully if enough people can identify the ways they're being controlled, things will change.

Run by the CIA and put into action during the 1950's, Project MKULTRA, or MK-ULTRA was the code name for an illegal operation performed covertly by the Office of Scientific Intelligence. This project was a human research program where US and Canadian citizens were used as subjects. MK-ULTRA was a dark chapter for the CIA: a barrage of torturous methods was used to alter brain functions in test subjects. Some examples of the methods used included heavy doses of experimental drugs, isolation, sexual abuse, and exposure to other chemicals. As the CIA mentally broke human beings with drugs and abuse, Congress finally stepped in in 1975. A Presidential commission known as the Rockefeller Commission was developed and both it and the Church Committee performed thorough investigations.

As can be expected with the CIA, the Director, Richard Helms, ordered all files related to MK-ULTRA to be destroyed in 1973. Some documents were recovered but much of the investigations were based on testimonials from either program administration that plead a deal for information or from test subjects of the program. By '77, a Freedom of Information Act (FOIA) request revealed a huge file of over 20,000 documents related to MK-ULTRA and as of recently, most information regarding the project has been declassified.

The CIA maintains that MK-ULTRA and other related types of human experimentation have been stopped, yet other versions of the story exist. Victor Marchetti, a 14 year veteran of the CIA has been interviewed about the CIA numerous times; nearly every interview he makes mention that the CIA regularly issue disinformation campaigns *and* that mind control research was still pursued by the CIA after the MK-ULTRA project. In an interview in '77, Marchetti identified the CIA response to their program being under scrutiny as a "cover story".

To give you a scope of techniques used in the MK-ULTRA project, in 1967 they rushed off to Canada because they knew that Congress would catch wind of them soon, and they brought in Dr. D. Ewen Cameron, a guy famous for drugging patients and subjecting them to the same word or phrase on repeat for hours. This is what he called, "treatment". From drug administration to administering heavy doses of psychological trauma upon patients, nothing was off limits for these experiments. Documents recovered about the project include a list of goals for test medications including paralysis, mental retardation and enhanced mental acuity and awareness. Over ten MILLION dollars went to this project during a time when the value of the dollar was still linked to the value of gold. Electrotherapy at 40 times the recommended power, LSD administration, sensory deprivation by forcing people into tiny cells without bathrooms and only mashed bugs to eat, waterboarding, hypnosis, and a paper trail to back it up is the legacy of the MK-ULTRA project. Both the US and Canadian governments settled out of court with 127 victims of the project for $100,000 each. Among those was the author of *One Flew Over the Cuckoo's Nest*, Kim Kesey, a godfather of LSD proliferation in the 60's. In short, not only were the mind experiments performed in MK-ULTRA dangerous to the participants, they also had the unintended side effect of exacerbating the drug-using, hippy culture of the 60's; the same counterculture that spurred the cannabis reform movement of today that the government still represses.

Most importantly to know, these MK-ULTRA experiments were conducted on both willing and unwilling test subjects and they resulted in at least one death that was ruled to be homicide, presumably as a result of a government operation. Anyone is fair game, anytime.

The Russian Sleep Experiment

Note – this story is a legend but it has grounds as many mind control experiments were conducted in Russia in the late 40's and early 50's, prompting the US to respond with experiments including the MK Ultra Project.

Russian military researchers in the late 1940s kept five human test subjects awake for fifteen [15] days using an experimental, gas-based stimulant. They were locked in a sealed containment facility to rigorously monitor their oxygen intake so that the gas wouldn't kill them: it was toxic in too high of a concentration. This experiment was conducted before closed circuit cameras, so the researchers used microphones and observed from a few 5-inch thick glass porthole sized windows into the room. The room was stocked with books, cots on which to sleep on but no bedding, running water and a toilet, and enough dried food to last all five for over a month.

The test subjects were all political prisoners deemed enemies of the State while fighting in World War II.

Everything was normal for the five first days: the subjects barely complained, too, having been falsely promised that they'd be freed if they submitted, and didn't sleep for 30 days. Their activities were monitored.

They began to talk about traumatic incidents in their past towards the end of the first few days and the whole tone of their conversations took on a much darker tone after the 4th day.

After five days, the war prisoners started to gripe about the events that led them to where they were. They started to demonstrate severe episodes of paranoia. They stopped talking to each other. They started alternately whispering to the microphones and one way mirrored portholes. Strangely, they all had it in their heads that they would win the trust of the experimenters if they only turned over their comrades, the other subjects in captivity with them. At first, researchers believed this was an effect of only the gas.

At the nine day mark, the first of the prisoners started screaming. He ran up and down the chamber repeatedly screaming at the top of his lungs. For three [3] hours straight he continued trying to scream but was only able to produce occasional squeaks. The researchers guessed that he'd probably torn his vocal cords. The surprising thing was how the other subjects reacted to the event, or rather didn't react to it. They kept whispering into the microphones until the next of the captives began screaming. The two quiet captives began tearing pages out of the books and smearing page after page with their own excrement, using it as paste to cover the view from the portholes. Once the portholes were covered, the screaming immediately stopped.

As did the whispering into the microphones.

Once three [3] more days passed, the researchers that had been checking the microphones every hour to ensure their working order, began thinking it was impossible that no sounds could have come from the room with five people inside. The oxygen consumption in the chamber indicated that all five were still alive, and, in fact, a higher than normal amount of oxygen was being consumed — similar levels to those of people doing strenuous exercise. The 14th morning, the military researchers did what they said they wouldn't do to get a reaction from the captives: they used the intercom and spoke into the chamber. Their fear was that all subjects were either dead or mentally dead.

They said to the subjects, "We're opening the doors to test the microphones - step away from the doors and lie flat on the floor or we WILL shoot you. Follow the instructions and one of you will be freed."

Startlingly, they heard a calm voice respond, "We no longer want to be freed."

Debate ensued between the researchers and the military hierarchy that was funding the research. Unable to get any further responses using the intercom, it was decided to open the chamber at midnight on the fifteenth [15] day.

The chamber was aired out so all stimulant gas was vacated. As the room began filling with fresh air, immediately voices came onto the microphone to object. Three different voices were begging, as though pleading for the life of loved ones, to turn on the gas again. The chamber doors were opened and soldiers went in to retrieve the human subjects. The subjects screamed louder than ever and so did the soldiers when they saw what was inside. Four out of the five subjects were "alive", though the state that any of them were found in hardly constitutes "life."

The food rations beyond day five had not been touched. There were chunks of fatty, oversaturated flesh and gore from the dead test subject's thighs and chest found stuffed into an overflowing drain that had allowed four inches of water to accumulate on the floor. Exactly how much was water and how much was blood wasn't determined. All four "surviving" subjects had large gouges of muscle and skin ripped away from their bodies. The type of destruction of flesh paired with the exposed bone at their fingertips indicated that their wounds were inflicted by hand; not with teeth as the researchers had initially postulated. More thorough examination of the positioning and angles of the wounds indicated that most of them, if not all of them, were self-inflicted.

The abdominal organs below the subjects' ribcages were removed. Though the heart, lungs and diaphragm remained in place, the skin and most muscles attached to the ribs had been torn off, exposing the subjects' lungs through their ribcages. All organs remained intact; they had just been taken out and laid upon the floor, haphazardly sitting around the eviscerated yet still living bodies of the subjects. The digestive tracts of all four were seen working, digesting food, while strewn about in front of the subjects. It quickly was apparent that **what** they were digesting was their own flesh that they tore off over the course of days.

Most of the soldiers stationed at this research project were Russian special operatives. Still, many refused to return to the chamber to remove the test subjects. The subjects continued to scream to be left in the chamber and both begged and demanded that the gas be turned back on – or else they would fall asleep.

To everyone's astonishment, the test subjects fought tooth and nail in the process of being removed. One Russian soldier died from having his throat torn out. Another was gravely injured by having his testicles torn off and an artery in his leg was severed by one subject's teeth. Another five soldiers lost their lives, if you count the ones that committed suicide in the weeks following.

During the struggle, one of the four living subjects ruptured his spleen and he bled out almost immediately. The researchers attempted to sedate him before his spleen was burst, but this proved impossible. He was injected with over ten times the normal dose of a morphine derivative and he still fought like a cornered animal, breaking the arm and ribs of one doctor. When his heart was seen to beat for a full two minutes after he had bled out, it was assumed that more air was running in his vascular system than blood. Even after his heart stopped, he continued to scream and flail for another three minutes, trying desperately to attack anyone within reach. He just repeated the word "MORE" over and over, till the cry got weaker and weaker, until he finally fell silent.

The surviving three subjects were restrained and moved to a medical facility. The two with working vocal cords continuously begged for the gas, demanding to be kept awake.

The most injured of the subjects was taken to the only surgical operating room in the facility. During the process of prepping the subject to have his organs put back in his body, it was found that he was indeed, effectively underline immune to the sedative they had to prepare him for surgery. He fought wickedly against the restraints when they doctors brought anesthetic gas to put him under. He actually tore most of the way through a four [4] inch wide leather strap on one of his wrists, even though the weight of a two-hundred [200] pound soldier was bracing that wrist down. It took only a little more anesthetic gas than normal to put him under. The instant his eyelids fluttered and closed, his heart stopped beating. In the autopsy of the test subject that died on the operating table it was found that his blood had triple the typical level of oxygen in it. His muscles that were still attached to his skeleton were badly torn and he had broken nine bones in his struggle. Most of the injuries were from the force that his own muscles had exerted.

The second survivor had been the first of the group to start screaming. His vocal cords were destroyed and he was unable to beg or object to surgery. He only reacted by shaking his head violently in disapproval when the anesthetic gas was brought over. He shook his head, "yes" when someone suggested that they try the surgery without anesthetic. He did not react for the entire six [6] hour procedure of replacing his abdominal organs and attempting to cover them with what remained of his skin. The surgeon stated repeatedly that it shouldn't be medically possible for the patient to still be alive. One terrified nurse assisting the surgery confessed that she had seen the patients mouth curl into a smile several times whenever she looked at him.

When the surgery ended, the subject looked at the surgeon and wheezed loudly, trying to talk, but struggling with his torn vocal chords. Assuming this must be something of importance, the surgeon had a pen and pad brought over so the patient could write his message. It was simple. "Keep cutting."

The other two test subjects were given the same surgery, both without anesthetic. They had to be injected with a paralytic for the operation because the surgeon found it unnerving to perform the operation while the patients uncontrollably laughed as he cut. Once paralyzed, the subjects could barely even follow the researchers with their eyes. The paralytic cleared out of their system in record time and they were quickly attempting to escape again. The minute they could speak, they were pleading for the stimulant gas. The researchers tried questioning them as to why they'd injured themselves... why they had ripped out their guts and why they wanted to be given the gas again.

Only one response was given by all subjects, "I must remain awake."

All three of the subjects' restraints were reinforced and they were placed back into the chamber awaiting word on what should be done. The researchers, facing the wrath of their military superiors for having failed the goals of their project, considered killing the remaining subjects. The commanding officer, who was an ex-KGB, saw potential and wanted to see what would happen if they were put **back** on the gas. The researchers strongly opposed this idea, but they were overruled and outranked.

To prepare for being sealed in the chamber again, the subjects were this time connected to an EEG monitor and they had their restraints padded for long term confinement. Sure enough, all three stopped struggling the moment they discovered that they were going back on the gas. It was obvious that at this point all three were struggling to stay awake. One of subjects that could speak was humming loudly and continuously; the mute subject was flexing his legs against the leather bonds with all his strength, first left, then right, then left again for something on which to focus. The remaining subject was lifting his head off of his pillow and blinking quickly in succession. Having been the first to get wired for EEG, most of the researchers were monitoring his brain waves at this point. His brainwaves were normal most of the time, but sometimes they flat-lined inexplicably. It looked like he was repeatedly suffering the death of his brain, then popping back to normal. As the examiners focused on paper scrolling out of the brainwave monitor, only one nurse saw his eyes slip shut. His brainwaves immediately changed to that of deep sleep, then they flat-lined for the last time as his heart stopped.

The last remaining subject that could speak began screaming to be sealed in immediately. His brainwaves showed the same flat-lines as the one who had just died after falling asleep. The commander gave the order to seal the chamber with both remaining subjects inside, as well as three [3] researchers. One of the three researchers immediately drew his gun and shot the commander in the head. He then turned the gun on the mute subject and blew his brains out.

He pointed his gun at the remaining subject. "I won't be locked in here with these things! Not with you!" he screamed at the dying man strapped to the table. "WHAT ARE YOU?" he demanded.

The subject smiled.

"Have you forgotten already?" The subject asked. "We are you. We are the madness that lurks inside you all, begging to be free at every moment in your deepest, animal mind. We are what you hide from in your beds every night. We are what you sedate into silence and paralysis when you go to the nocturnal haven where we cannot tread."

The researcher paused. Then aimed at the subject's heart and fired. The EEG flat-lined as the subject weakly choked out, "So... nearly... free..."

Fluoridated Water

Drinking water: it's often found bottled at a charge lately, but there was a day when hose water and faucet water were sources of cool, liquid refreshment on a hot day. Ice cubes are made from the faucet typically, and we all shower using our local water supply. What isn't overtly mentioned is the fact that our clean water supply is mixed with a low content of industrial-grade fluoride. When investigated, it turns out that the US was the first to implement widespread fluoridation of public water supply and that only a few other countries and continents have as high exposure as the USA.

Published in 1978,

"The first occurrence of fluoridated drinking water on Earth was found in Germany's Nazi prison camps. The Gestapo had little concern about fluoride's supposed effect on children's teeth; their alleged reason for mass-medicating water with sodium fluoride was to sterilize humans and force the people into their concentration camps into calm submission."

The Crime and Punishment of I.G. Farben by Joseph Borkin

From this passage, it's clear where the US got the idea of water fluoridation from – Nazi scientists that made their way into government laboratories after World War II. With test results confirming that fluoride prevented tooth decay, the mind-numbing and sterilizing effects were never made part of the "official script". Fluoride is also proven to be harmful to humans. A coalition of medical professionals called the Institute for Science in Medicine, (ISM) published a counter-propaganda piece called, "The Anti-Fluoridationist Threat to Public Health", published in 2012. It scathes at many health professionals that claim fluoride can be damaging, as well as at the advertising tactics of the anti-fluoridation lobby. While some points are well found, the document does not address the link between thyroid failure and fluoride found presented in a 2006 study by the US National Research Council. There are also concerns about links to cancer and other illnesses. Twenty-four [24] studies have been conducted including some from Mexico that show an association between exposure to fluoride and reduced IQ.

Europe has banned water fluoridation and among countries, the US, Brazil and Australia are the most notorious for fluoridated water. Just knowing that Nazis studied the effects of fluoride and put it in their camp water according to a reliable source knowledgeable about the forerunning German chemical company, I.G. Farben, should make it obvious that the US is not fluoridating the water solely for the benefit of reducing tooth decay.

GMO Foods

Despite being banned in Europe and progressively more Asian countries, GMO's, aka: Genetically Modified Organisms, are a US super pseudo-science specialty. Introduced to the States in 1996, GMO's take the form of all types of foods at the grocery store: tomatoes, pickles, microwaveable meals and if current research is any indicator, someday there will be GMO meat portions. Despite a drastic increase in chronic illness and food allergies from 1996 – 2005, no Federal ban has been considered regarding GMO's in the States. Both the American Public Health Association and the American Nurses Association oppose the use of GMO's, especially in the use of bovine (cow) hormones. Apparently, genetically modified bovine growth hormones exist that bulk cows up so they produce more milk. Unfortunately, treated cows also leave heavy deposits of the IGF-1 hormone, (an insulin-like growth compound) which is definitively cancer-causing.

Supreme reigning monopoly of the genetically modified organism game is the company Monsanto. This company has been giving and taking so much money to the government that it may as well be the National Bank of Monsanto. Truth is, it's actually a much scarier institution. Monsanto is working to bio-engineer insect and weather resistant crops, then they demand payment for the new seeds from farmers. If farmers refuse to use the seeds, Monsanto has been known to sue farmers for having Monsanto copyrighted crops on their fields after either spillage occurs from neighboring farms that did opt for Monsanto's products OR, in some cases, Monsanto has been known to covertly spread seed into land of farmers that refused to buy GMO seeds and then file legal proceedings.

What could be so important about GMO's that the US government is willing to trade its citizens' health for mass proliferation of offending crops and seeds? It's been well documented in lab rat studies that GMO's cause tumors and a vast array of terminal health concerns in as little as a single generation. The FDA doesn't even require labeling of GMO products so consumers are left to educate themselves. In truth, know that GMO's cause illness and that if our government is fluoridating our water, they quite possibly could be genetically engineering our food to pacify and control us.

Anti-Cannabis Rhetoric

Cannabis is among the most symbiotic plants for humans on Earth. It can be made into medicines that cure illnesses across a huge spectrum, including cancer and other previously incurable diseases. It has suffered slander and propaganda that bastardized it as a "drug" when in fact the USA was poised to be the largest producer of cannabis not long before the prohibition of it in 1938. Originally, Henry Ford designed his cars' engines to run on hemp fuel. He also made the paneling out of hemp fiber. To demonstrate the hardiness of the paneling, Ford was known to smack the car paneling with his cane as hard as possible. No dents, scratches or scuffs showed – compare that to if the car paneling of today were hit full force with a cane – the plastic would break for sure! Hemp is good to make clothing with and can be used as a base in concrete mixture called "hempcrete" which is naturally fire, mold and water resistant and significantly cheaper than stone concrete to produce. Long story short, cannabis is nothing but good for integration into human societies across the globe. For that same reason, it has been made illegal and it has been demonized to maintain the illusion that it is harmful.

Curing cancer, (note, not the cure for cancer, but the process of WORKING to cure it) is a billion dollar industry. Recent studies have shown THC literally killing cancer under high microscopic observation. If cannabis cures cancer, the mainstream proliferation of evidence of this would mean that cancer research would stop being funded. It would spell disaster to the healthcare industry that relies heavily on terminal illness in order to stay profitable. As a form of mind control, the government is knowingly keeping a phenomenal medicine away from patients, and they have been doing so since the 1970's. Yes, the US Government knew in the 70's after the issuance of the Shaeffer Report, that cannabis was mostly harmless and actually showed medicinal potential.

Lastly, think of the typical "stoner" caricature – they are lazy, dirty, smelly, hippy-type individuals with blazing red eyes, a slow reaction time and who are always hungry. Just the same way as we used to call the Vietcong, "Charley" or "chinks", just the same way that generations of white racists have kept blacks down by perpetuating the "n word" and with exactly the same hateful disgust as when gay bashers would call innocent men "faggots" before beating them to death, the stereotypical image of a stoner is false and insulting. Cannabis users include people from every socio-economic bracket within the United States. Poor to super rich all partake in cannabis use. Organizations such as NORML have been founded to change bad laws and fight for the integrity of the people who use cannabis as a medicine or recreationally. Still, according to Federal law in the US and in most other countries, if you are caught with cannabis, you are breaking the law.

Never has there been a more brazen mind control program over the free-will of the citizenship since alcohol prohibition. While alcohol prohibition lasted a mere thirteen [13] years, cannabis prohibition has been a social experiment lasting over seventy-five years [75]. It seems as though angry, fitting adult-babies with machine guns achieved their goal of ending prohibition much quicker than well-thought arguments provided by peaceful protesters. Nonetheless, if Martin Luther King Jr. could lead African Americans into a new dawn of civil rights through peaceful protest, clearly peaceful protest will work to shed light on the benefits of cannabis, the dangers of prohibition and the rightful place of government – out of your life and especially out of your mind and decision-making.

Experiments In Military Telekinesis, Telepathy And Mind Warfare

Similarly to the inspiration behind pursuing projects like MK ULTRA in mind control, the US also caught wind of Russian and Chinese ESP and "remote viewing" projects that led them to follow suit. US Government studies into the psychic abilities of soldiers originated out of World War II, but got significant and traceable funding starting in the '70's.

While testing a subject for potential as a "remote viewer", aka: someone clairvoyant or able to predict the future or see things that were concealed using mental instinct, Harold Puthoff, a privately funded researcher working at Stanford Research Institute, (SRI) was visited by two CIA employees who struck a deal for a $50,000 project.

On concept alone, the project was renewed and given broader depth. CIA officials including John N. McMahon, who headed the Office of Technical Service and eventually became the CIA Deputy Director, were largely in support of this program. This was the birth of what became known as Project STARGATE, a decades long attempt of the US Government to identify and use psychically-attuned individuals for intelligence gathering during and for war.

Operating under different branches and names from 1972 to 1995, Project Stargate reported success in finding individuals with above-average cognition. It was claimed that 65% accuracy on tests of clairvoyance, (the measure mark of whether such a phenomenon as telepathy could exist) was being hit and surpassed by subjects. Despite increasingly positive results, when the story was made public in 1984, criticism from the National Academy of Sciences National Research Council spurred heavy review of the program which led to smaller and smaller budgets, eventually leading to the project's demise in 1995.

Growing Police State- Fear Mongering In The USA

As recently as August, 2014, the United States has seen examples of how a Police State rises in lieu of protests against the same old racist, classist and elite-serving policies that have existed and perpetuated over the course of hundreds of years. September 11th is a date forever etched into the brains of Americans – it was when, according to the State scripted reports, terrorists attacked us domestically for the first time since Pearl Harbor. What that date represents differs for all of us. Most of us can agree that we saw a forfeit of some simple rights. More thorough searches at airports, for existence, or the creation of agencies such as the TSA and Homeland Security all pointed to 9/11 as full warrant for their newly given authority. Increases in school shootings spawned civilian and government task forces dedicated to responding to such events. Earlier in 2014, the Boston Marathon Bombing tragedy resulted in police searches of entire neighborhoods for the suspect: warrantless searches that breached Constitutionally ensured rights.

Subconsciously, the increased presence of military forces, either in the form of police that are outfitted in military gear, or the ACTUAL military as was the case in Ferguson, MO in August, certainly affects the masses. Creating a society ruled by fear is a key element of control; while police and military are sworn to defend and protect the American people, it is often the American government responsible for the offenses and encroachments upon individual liberty. Mind control can be as simple as purveying the image that the US police force is stronger than any public uprising.

In the US, instances of global fear-mongering are often covered in order to make the public feel better about circumstances here. For instance, major outlet coverage of the arrest of the Russian protest rock group, Pussy Riot, led to many televised debates about the difference in freedom between the Russians and our people. In reality, a similar flash mob, protest group would just as swiftly be arrested and prosecuted in NYC, Philadelphia or any other large city. Recently, for example, Philadelphia hosted events at the Liberty Bell called Smoke Down Prohibition events. These were mass forms of protest against illogical cannabis law. After several months of unchecked freedom to hold the events, Park Rangers and Federal agents raided an event in the spring and arrested N.A. Poe, the organizer, as well as an internet personality and host, Adam Kokesh. Most protesters were not cited and protests continued after the arrests, but they soon fizzled out due to the public's fear of prosecution. These events were a page taken out of the book of the Occupy Movement, which began at Wall Street and spread quickly throughout the country in 2011.

Omnipresent Surveillance State

Have you ever gotten the feeling that you're being watched? This used to be a key element of suspense in a world where global surveillance didn't exist. As recently as a couple of decades ago, it was highly unlikely that the government could be monitoring you from the clouds along with everyone else you know and love. One example of paranoia about the surveillance state in mainstream culture is in the movie, *Goodfellas*, when the main character is driving to deliver guns to a fellow mobster and notices a black helicopter following throughout his day of "errands" to run for the mob. Today, surveillance is a reality that Edward Snowden helped us understand. Our State is unchecked in its use of surveillance technology and it does not reserve the data collection and monitoring to specific, hostile targets. Citizens are tapped, in more ways than they think.

Drivers locations are recorded through EZPass stations, GPS's and cell phones. Individuals are tracked by their phones and can be identified within a few meters, unless they don't carry a smartphone. Even without a phone, individuals can be tracked by US spy drones that operate 70-80,000 feet in the air, but can zoom and record your daily events close enough to spot acne on your face, or food stains on your shirt. Days of CIA spy work on the ground and dreams of super suave spy agents like James Bond have quickly been replaced by the allure of people using simulators that operate very similarly to a video game to spy on everyday people.

Psychologically, the existence of a surveillance state will affect individual behavior. Those that are aware that technology has made it virtually impossible to evade surveillance will be less inclined to commit major crimes. They can often feel trapped, or anxious. Since the dawn of man, privacy has been valued, whether during bathroom time or time for intimacy. Privacy has also aided the manufacturing of most drugs on the market and abetted countless millions of cases of domestic abuse. Regardless of whether eliminating privacy as a comfort of life will prevent domestic abuse, drug abuse or violence against the State, privacy is a core element of freedom and eliminating it is the equivalent of making us all into lab rats in a cage, under 24/7 monitoring.

Government- Big Pharmaceuticals Backscratching- Opiating The Masses

Merck, Pfizer and the countless Universities and Colleges that perform medical research and development are all guilty of suppressing cures in place of "treatments". While the government mandates healthcare, drug companies are getting subsidized ever growing amounts for the psyche-altering pills that they dispense. Ritalin and Adderall are merely methamphetamine type stimulants. Pain medication is almost always opiate-based. By prescribing mentally and physically addictive substances to children as young as six years old, our healthcare system in the US is doing as much to create the drug problem as the government is to eradicate it.

Most instances of opiate addiction start due to a prescription for opiate-based painkillers either after surgery or a major injury. While the government knows that there are safer alternative pain killers, opiate-based medication has become the standard for the effectiveness of the pain relief. Also suspect in this equation is the fact that Afghanistan is the leader of the world when it comes to poppy cultivation. Through imperialistic conquest, the US has invaded a country rich in both oil and the crop necessary to produce the pain medication of domestic choice. Even within the past year, an initiative to re-schedule cannabis was rejected while the FDA approved a new opiate pain reliever that is extremely potent and extremely easy for addicts to abuse. Economics and oligarchies continue to repress the population at large, hugely without concern for the public interest. In the pharmaceuticals game, this is best demonstrated by the State exclusive access to Naloxone, the injection that pulls someone out of an opiate overdose. Addicts will get treated, so long as they submit to the State for processing – otherwise, they're just another urchin found dead in the streets.

Without question, the government has a vested interested in a drugged population – if not opiated, then drugged with stimulants or depressants of the legal variety. When people are drugged, they are susceptible to mind control easier. Mental acuity diminishes in the presence of alcohol, caffeine, opiates or cocaine. People still function, they just don't thrive. Neither do they rise up against the system of control over them. If anything, heavily drugged people become *part* of the system, increasing the numbers in the Prison Industrial complex. Especially given the surge of prescriptions to kids for stimulant-based medications, it is obvious that our government aims to control us through drugs. This is also part of the reason why drugs like cannabis, mushrooms and LSD are illegal – they open the mind to different thinking that flies in the face of traditional wisdom and they risk the population developing as a charitable community rather than a private-interest competition. Nonetheless, hard drug abuse, whether prescribed or illegal, is asking to be taken for the proverbial "ride". Clear thinking leads to informed decision-making and a sharp wit, resilient against mind attacks such as subliminal messaging in commercials.

The College Lie

Everyone has heard the spiel by the time they're in the 11th grade: "you need to get into a good college or you won't have as many opportunities later in life!" While this is generally a true statement, it is also a loaded statement. It implies that for the next four or more years of your life, you will be accumulating tens of thousands, if not hundreds of thousands of dollars in debt. Some kids get into the colleges of their dreams but can't afford it. Others ride the coattails of their alumni parents and earn success and fortune through a legacy of average grades and ideas, (George W. Bush, for example). College is supposed to prepare students for a career in the field in which they studied. What it seems more apt for lately is being the stepping stone towards different dreams of over-institutionalized individuals. Only the laser-focused super-tasking individuals capable of double full-time work loads can effectively navigate through doctoral programs. Even these incredible individuals often get punished for their years of hard work in the form of medical malpractice insurance premiums and high tax brackets courtesy of the IRS. While many see this as being, "just the way of things", our entertainers and our sports heroes make anywhere from double to more than ten times as much as these unsung martyrs of medicine. With such incredible stratification between stratospheric socio-economic classes, it leaves the poor to wonder if there's any hope of securing even the five basic essentials of life:

- Water

- Food

- Shelter

- Clothing

- Love

- Being poor used to be seen as a special Hell reserved for those that were lazy and disingenuous. Now in light of record unemployment and no new middle class paying jobs, a huge portion of the student population is sliding down from the Middle Class status of their parents deep into poverty when faced with the challenges of surviving alone. Even Bachelor's degree holders are finding themselves working for $9-$10 per hour for years without raise or promotion. Perhaps college is a "must", but should it be a "must" in order to have a minimum wage position?

- Student loans are at an all-time, blazingly high level. *The Economist* published in June 2014 that student loan debts in the United States alone exceeded 1.2 trillion dollars [$1,200,000,000,000] and that over seven million borrowers were currently in default for their loans. If the US were to consider that entire amount "bad debt", it would increase the total US

National Debt by nearly 7% in an instant. Clearly, the jobs that these students were "preparing for" in college didn't exist, therefore leading to many students surviving on minimum wage and low-earning jobs, left unable to repay their loans. Currently, the percentage of children in low-income working families is on the rise – between 2008 – 2012, there were 1.6 million more 13-18 year old kids in low income homes. Numbers of kids between 6 and 13 years old who are living in low income working families has increased by 1.1 million in the same time frame. Perhaps an indicator that times have been getting harder, fewer younger children have been coming up into poverty, with only an increase of 300,000 kids from infancy to 6 being raised in low income families. Data from 2012-2014 is expected to continue the trend of increasing numbers of low income families, unable to pay for food on their tables let alone student loan debt. In a recent, April 2014 Millennial Jobs Report published by *Generation Opportunity*, a non-partisan youth advocacy group found that the jobless rate for 18-29 year olds stands at 15.5%, well above the 6.2% national average for unemployment. This is just further proof that collectively, parents in the US and across the globe are blindly pushing their children into a debt trap that has no exit.

- The original intent of exclusivity in colleges and universities remains the same; those with the tightest knit collection of alumni friends, frat brothers and sorority sisters are those that network into wealth the easiest. Those who earn degrees online or those that focus solely on their studies and jobs get stuck in dead end jobs or slow-advancing career paths. They will struggle in large numbers while the few families that fund Harvard, Yale and Princeton will find CEO, CFO, and other executive, six-figure salaried starting positions.

- **Being afforded a greater lot in life for having been through 2-6 years of an accredited educational establishment is a ploy to enroll record numbers of students into college at a time when tuition has increased over 1,000% in the past 100 years and when a single book alone can cost upwards of $400.**

- Colleges also are notorious for loving players that get them paid. Economically, a school that is well-known for a phenomenal sports team invests majority stakes into the development and maintenance of that team. Take for example the sex abuse conviction of Jerry Sandusky and the Penn State sanctions that followed: a University was crippled because of massive fines directed at a huge profit machine for their establishment.

- While on the topic of college sports, player abuse – both physically and financially are very real in higher academic institutions. College players receive no compensation for their likenesses and appearances in video games and broadcasts while their Universities and Colleges make millions. This has led to lawsuits and minor reform on the part of education administration officials regarding compensation of student athletes. Physical abuse is rampant as well – in 2013, a Rutgers basketball coach, Mike Rice was fired for hitting, kicking and calling his players anti-gay slurs. Still, the show must go on, as hundreds of millions of fans nationally across every sport rely on their seasonal entertainment.

- It is in part because of the huge emphasis on sports that fanaticism runs rampant and drives nationalism and local pride. In the USA as well as many other cultures such as Germany, Ireland, England and Australia, a drinking culture has pervaded the youth and just recently legally allowed to drink. In capitalist driven, first-world companies, marketing ploys rely on sex appeal, social acceptance and all the classic conventions of marketing to get drinks into the hands of people at any age possible. Remember that within the past 100 years, the drinking age was raised by each State from 18 to 21, greatly at the behest of the Federal Government reacting after a failed Prohibition of alcohol. Excess and partying became integrated into the youthful culture and competition soon became just as much a social experiment as was practice on the field.

- Those that may not have partied hard or pursued professional careers in their given sport may have done what so many do in times of need; they enlist. Coming right out of a sports environment where competition and pushing your physical and mental limits is ingrained in daily life, the military receives scores if not thousands of ready-made soldiers coming directly from High Schools. Given the revealed government concern for the free-will of others, these 18 year old, impressionable young adults can more readily be indoctrinated. Recent controversy concerning questionnaires issued by the military concerning whether or not soldiers would be willing to kill American citizens if they refused to surrender their arms under new Federal law goes to show that our government is always working to create soldiers more loyal to the State than to the people that they are sworn to defend from all threats, domestic and foreign.

- For the kids that may not have excelled in sports or academia, there is always the popular option of further institutionalization, either in form of prison or a mental health complex. Schools are remarkably like prisons: many have concrete walls, there is often a Security presence, especially since 9/11 and in lieu of inner-city violence, and it is a strictly regulated, time-budgeted form of brainwashing. Negative reinforcement exists such as detention and suspension, which is often seen as a vacation to the misguided student, repressed by a well-oiled, government institution for all. From here, it is a slippery slope to disciplinary school referrals, academic probation, juvenile hall, and ultimately, jail.

- Another similarity between schools and jail is the horrible food, in horrible portions. As a part of Michelle Obama's MOVE! Agenda, school meals must meet certain nutritious requirements in order to be allowed in the cafeteria. This has led to mal-nourished kids who refuse to eat the "healthy" fruit cocktails and meager portions of grilled chicken over rice. Marriot and other school food providers are unsurprisingly also partnered with prisons for food. Marriot was recently fined for a number of health code violations in their prison food. Inmates complained of maggots in the food and they weren't lying. One other thing that is almost certain about Marriot – they do not discriminate between GMO products versus those that were organic-grown.

- In the early 2000's, High School cafeteria food was different. At my school in suburbia, we had a vast assortment of options including burgers, fries, cheese fries, pizza, hoagies, soda and even tacos. Sure, cheese fries may not be "healthy" but kids would eat them. It would sustain them in the case that all they had packed was an apple and a tuna fish sandwich. Now, these food options are surely banned as a result of Michelle Obama. Personally, I can't tell which is worse – a fast food culture or a prison food culture.

- An obvious form of mind control in schools is nationalist indoctrination, starting at the age of six [6]. Beginning in Kindergarten, children are taught the Pledge of Allegiance. "I pledge allegiance, to the Flag of the United States of America, and to the Republic for which it stands, one nation under God, indivisible, with liberty and justice for all." This is said daily before class and has been part of national school policy for decades. Even procedures as innocuous as fire drills are a form of conditioning for the masses in case of catastrophe. Due to terrorist activity in the past twenty years, the Federal Government has even created new drills including Terrorist Attack drills and some schools have drills for evacuation in case of gun fire.

- On the rise in the US are school shootings where students snap under the pressure of social and academic expectations paired with an unstable mental condition. In most recent cases of school shootings, there have been links argued that all shooters had been prescribed some sort of anti-depressant or anti-anxiety pill. Whether there is a correlation has yet to be determined. What is definitive is that the frequency of these attacks is not subsiding; then again, neither has the mentality in response to such an event. Mainstream media uses the event as an opportunity to lobby for or against gun control while mental health laws sit and die in Congress.

- Some would say that these events are on the rise because of an increasingly violence tolerant public. Between news and entertainment channels, violence is reported on or visualized on television daily and sometimes hourly for some people. What this does to the psyche of a susceptible mind is questionable, though all tests point to violence being inherent within a personality versus being conditioned through media.

- Genetics are part of what make us unique. Every person has their own pattern and it either serves or detriments them. More aggressive individuals may be predisposed to violence because of their genes. What was nature's way of ensuring that the fittest survive by painting broad swaths of personalities has become a nightmarish prison world for minds hardly capable of understanding what is happening to them, in some cases. By no means does this mean that sociopathic and psychotic killers do not exist, it does mean though, that these people may have been programmed as a Venus Fly Trap among flies in their head. If the government didn't benefit by having this free, (or sometimes staged) press, it wouldn't make national news. That is why the source of the problem isn't addressed, and why reactionary responses from government figures often leads to a debate about a similar topic like gun control or expanding the police state.

- Sometimes school shootings occur because students are suffering from a mental condition like depression or schizophrenia. It may have been latent, but signs usually present themselves before a fatal event. If a student is feeling like they are losing in an "unwinnable" fight, they are more susceptible to thoughts of suicide – thoughts of suicide and thoughts of homicide can be closely linked. Rage and anger are often associated with depression. Those that enact their rage on others are clearly and always disturbed individuals but with a more effective social safety net, their pain wouldn't have to be the pain of many innocent families. Largely, lack of communication or connection with family, a hatred for institutionalization and authoritative repression and underlying mental illness contribute parts of a larger answer that has yet to be understood. Maybe if schools weren't like jails, (and if jails weren't deplorable), students and inmates would stop being unhappy and wanting to end their lives. Where's the Pre-Emptive Counselling for clearly disturbed children? If the school isn't qualified to handle cases of mentally disturbed individuals, why aren't kids getting timely referrals to Institutes that could help? One potential answer is,

The government needs status quo tragedies to fuel its' image as compassionate towards its' people, even though they were proven to be testing mind control on unwitting subjects just under forty [40] years ago. There is no proof that any of the recent mass murder cases covered by the media were sleeper agents, though there have been rumors. Either way, forcing kids to adhere to up to ten [10] different, focused disciplines each day with limited time for social interaction and also subjecting them to stringent, social rules about smoking, drinking and public displays of affection can't help encourage budding personalities and newly in-love couples. They serve as a form of mind control — a way to maintain the status quo of abstinence and archaic values that don't represent all familial values or choices.

Neurolinguistic Programming (NLP)

Imagine having the ability to tell when people are lying; to tell when they remember something that is either fictional or concrete. Now imagine being able to use this ability to sway conversations towards your favor. This isn't science fiction, this is Neurolinguistic Programming, (NLP). Commonly taught to high level government officials as well as key unit members such as hostage negotiators, NLP is the practice of reading the eye patterns of others while using subtle mind tricks to win the subject's favor and extract information or a desired result.

In the 1970's, two men named John Grinder and Richard Bandler claimed to have found a direct link between neurology and language. They claimed that it could be exploited for psychological gain for subjects including overcoming phobias, treating psychosomatic illnesses as well as being able to reach people with learning disabilities. Today, NLP is highly integrated into sales and business culture and the government.

Critics of NLP have the upper hand when it comes to scientific review: numerous factual errors have been presented about NLP's foundational assertions, yet it remains taught to and used by professionals across a range of industries. Opponents of NLP claim it is a very superficial study into verbal/ nonverbal communication . They also claim that techniques like NLP are only popularized through commercialization. For instance, NLP is often discussed by those that run self-help seminars in their varying forms: personal development, business edge or attracting members of your preferred gender for intimacy are all included.

At its core, NLP is a simple process. First, you establish rapport with your subject. Match their vocal inflections and try to mimic them in a comfortable, non-obvious way. Be complimentary but not overly so. Next, it is important to understand "anchors". These are non-obvious gestures that can be used to "plant" an idea in the subject's head. It could be touching the leg of someone you want intimately or it could be placing a reassuring hand on the subject's shoulder... Often it is a physical contact if possible, as that makes the "anchor" stronger. Now understanding this, communication with a goal is established. Say you wanted to sell the subject your car. NLP teaches that through listening and asking guided questions, it's possible to direct any conversation towards your goal. This is accomplished by deepening the rapport with the subject by understanding what drives them. Below is a chart of eye patterns that NLP claims are reflectively of the majority of the population. It is often the case with left-handed people for this chart to be reversed in practical use.

Constructed memories are linked to when a person looks to their right, (your left). Upward eye patterns indicate a visual imagination where direct side eye movement indicates imagining audio, (what would it sound like if Mickey Mouse sung the national anthem?). Downwards looks to the right (your left) by the subject means that they are accessing their feelings, past or present. On the subject's left glance, (so you would see their eyes move to the right) it can be disseminated that the subject is accessing memories of either something visual or audio. Downwards eye movements in this direction are indicative of the subject having a mental dialogue. Through reading eye patterns after asking the subject guiding questions, the controller can bring the subject into a mental state simply through suggestion. Granted, the subject must be in a relaxed state, but given that and a skilled practitioner of NLP, it is possible to disseminate the exact thought pattern that the subject goes through when making a decision on just about anything: making a purchase, taking a risk, being very extraverted or introverted, etc.

By asking guiding questions about the subject's buying habits, what they like about cars and by anchoring emotional states, NLP allows the controller to fuel the subject's desire to buy a car before even mentioning that there is a car for sale. During the closing parts of the technique, at the height of the point of sale, anchors can be revisited, causing the subject to "toggle" back into excitability and thus make easier to control. Another crucial aspect of NLP is the use of keywords in dialogue when presenting guiding questions that speaks to the thought process of the subject. For instance, if the controller asks the subject what cars they like, and the subject looks up and to the left, (your right) it means there is a specific car that they're thinking of – they remembered a vision of a car. From this information, the controller would begin using the keywords "see", "seeing" "sight for sore eyes" etc. as well as focusing on how much the car they're selling "looks" like the subject's favorite car. Similarly, if the subject looked quickly sideways, auditory keywords would be used. "I like what I'm hearing", "heard", "loud" and other types of phrases could be used that would subconsciously attract the subject. NLP is all about reading the body language and eyes of whoever you are trying to manipulate and it is used in every day media such as tv commercials and print ads.

NLP may not be validated through neuroscience yet, however, the results speak for themselves. Success stories come from seminars and clinics where the goal is to make people more social, more sales ready or more likeable. NLP plays a major role in the development of certain hypnotic therapies, even today. Whether it has been proven to work is a moot point if the technique actually presents consistent results in the field. Given even the possibility that there is a pattern to linguistics that can make subjects submit information willingly, it is clear why the government would make use of this technique, both in teaching it to their top officials as well as integrating its use in training subservient loyalists, either in the military or the civilian cross-section of the public.

Conclusion

After evaluating the history of propaganda and how it developed into mind control through the use of repetition and military application, its guaranteed that elements of the former mind control projects live on in agencies and training reserved for specific roles in the military and government. Decades and millions of dollars went into research for projects like Stargate and MK ULTRA specifically: claiming that nothing was learned would be the epitome of denial. What is most likely is that the US government found information that it was looking for, covered up by destroying the records, but continuing research into elements of the project that worked somewhere else, with a new team. To this day, it is highly likely that the government: whether it's the CIA, NSA, Homeland Security or other, still perform pre-cognitive tests and still actively pursue a psy-ops program.

Recently, a new advancement has been made that allowed one subject, through use of a couple of medical devices hooked up to his head and hand, as *well* as the internet, was able to control another person's finger over the distance between their computers. By sensing brain patterns when the tester lifted his own finger, the observed patterns were sent to the subject – the pattern was duplicated through electro-magnetic resonance.

What the subject said, "felt like an urge" was the involuntary result of medical science meeting science fiction on the internet — now that it's proven that sensor devices paired with the internet can override will, how long until this technology is used for military or civilian control purposes?

Imagine the worst case scenario: it's only fifty [50] years in the future, pockets of resistance against the rogue government exist but are limited in resources and communication. In an effort to secure world dominance, the US Government develops human clone soldiers that are implanted with extremely powerful sensors. Through channels as readily available as cell signal and wifi, the US Government was able to control the clones using AI algorithms in a central supercomputer, designed to create an unbeatable military hive mind — every soldier fights till death, no soldier backs down or fails their mission. This is just fiction but with the advances in medical and technological breakthroughs that are being made, immediate uses for technology like this could include stimulating the brain of subjects being interrogated to yield truth unwillingly — or even worse — yield whatever reply that the interrogator desires.

Conspiracy theory does not run dry when dreaming about the present and future mind control experiments in the US and world. It has already been presented by some fringe domain owners that ELF towers, ELF standing for "Extremely Low Frequency". There are photos of strange towers that are often dismissed as "cell phone towers". In reality, the US Government has installed thousands of what are known as Ground Wave Emergency Network (GWEN) Towers across the States.

If you've ever seen a spire similar to the one pictured above, you have seen real government mind control devices already. These towers are designed to omit extremely low frequencies that have been used for crowd control in the past. In England, Greenpeace demonstrators reported skin burns, untimely menstrual bleeding, headaches and a multitude of other symptoms. They claimed they were being "irradiated". In actuality, ELF towers were put into use to disperse the crowd, yet the official government position was that the crowd was not targeted. All of the symptoms reported fit with overexposure to electromagnetic waves.

If the Government already has towers erected designed to disorient and physiologically disable mass areas, it is also then entirely within reason to believe that they would already be RFID chipping their citizens for tracking purposes. RFID, aka: Radio Frequency ID is a tiny chip that can be read using a radio receiving device. Some can only be read with a handheld scanner, but there are also battery-powered versions on the market that can be read up to five hundred feet away. Information is stored on a microchip inside of a small capsule or electronics housing, (depending on whether the device is an implant or not). What's scariest about this, is that while the RFID chip has a limited memory and thus, a limited amount of information that can be stored, given the availability of secure Government internet space, all that would be needed in your RFID chip is a web address – from there, the government could access information about your credit, your shopping habits, your kids, your marriages, your arrest record, your grades in school and just about any other bit of information there is to collect on you, (including your phone calls, texts and emails). Due to the availability of such information via information tracking done by major companies and government programs, (mass transit, driving privilege. gun registry, etc.) the Government has free reign to conduct massive intelligence gathering operations through the CIA. Now most people may shrug this off saying, "Well, they'd have to get a chip in me, and I KNOW I'm not chipped." How do you know?

What if you're bugged right now and you don't even know it? RFID chips are small – just five to ten years ago they could get them as small as a grain of rice. Today, it's possible that RFID self-assembling nano-bots exist. Imagine drinking a glass of water that has been spiked with a bug – the nano-bots assemble within your gut and stick to your stomach, all the while transmitting the information about you that could be useful to the government. Another common objection is, "Why would the government track me?" It's clear that you are not special to the government – if other people have been, why not you? Often times the government needs cross-sections for their covert studies that fit across a broad demographic. A painter. A delivery guy. A lawyer. A trust fund baby. They may not have anything to do with each other, but all of them may be under surveillance and not even know it.

Luckily, most veterinarians have the equipment to read RFID chips so if you're entirely convinced that you've been chipped, make friends with your local vet and ask politely after explaining the situation. If anything, they'll probably be excited to see if you're chipped, too. There are ways to check and prepare yourself against mind control and mass manipulation by your government.

Unfortunately, being informed and concerned makes you more suspect in this day and age. Be aware that even normal people could be subjects or unwilling participants in the experimentation of the covert programs in the US. Remember Edward Snowden's message that the spying is not refined to military or domestic threats. Remember the shocking admission that voyeur pictures obtained from spy drones and other surveillance technologies are spread inter-office at the CIA, NSA and Homeland Security. Don't settle for the FOX news version of life, or the MSNBC version because it's more "liberal". Remember that through all of the shiny faces in the morning and all of the entertainment acts, that it is just a ploy to maintain an established status quo.

Looking to the future, the probability of human error leading to rights abuses in lieu of such powerful surveillance and mind control is inevitable. It has already happened. What's scariest is the way that we are presently content. Generally, there is not pandemonium in the States and when riots and protests do occur, they are met with swift, civil justice. We have not united yet against things that we clearly should be against – unlimited spying, unwarranted search and seizure and so many other infractions. If the current rate of apathy and placidity continues, the future for mankind as we know it may be under constant surveillance. Sauron's "All Seeing Eye" may actually become a reality, and the Orcs and denizens may be the militarized cops and corrupt government officials hosting the gross parade.

Do not fall victim to the elements of control. Fight by drinking clean, un-fluoridated water. Fight by ingesting clean, organically grown foods. Fight back by spreading the truth of the atrocities done upon the People in the name of the Government. If we don't start bucking against mass control soon, then it may be proof that we're already too far controlled.

Once more, imagine that scenario where the government breeds human clone soldiers in tubes, devoid of personality and feeling yet controlled through sensors and remotes. Consider the ramifications of a society run by humanoid-machines, not totally unlike the "Terminator" series. When we have the technology to control others' minds remotely in labs, it is only a matter of time before we use technology to control minds on the battlefield. After that, it apparently only takes a year or two for the cops to get a hold of the technology. Then what? Cops with the ability to make people commit crimes? This concept sounds ludicrous but it's exactly the kind of rights breach that occurred in the PROJECT MK ULTRA starting in the '70's.

Beyond a shadow of a doubt, your government is lying to you and planning ways to make you a controllable asset more readily and stealthily. Arm yourself with knowledge. Shield yourself with wariness. Always question the things that happen in your life and always fight to say that you were the harbinger of either your success or your doom. When others control you to serve their purposes, it makes you a tool – a literal piece of handy machinery being used to make someone *just* like you more money, more famous, more glorified, etc. Don't do it. Stand up, assert your rights and protect your mind. We will see a revolution soon and when we do, it'll become obvious how well prepared our government is at repressing resistance to their control.

FREE BONUS

Binaural Beats
(Brain Frequencies)

Now that you've finished this book on how others are influencing you, we want to empower you. Head over to your internet browser and type in:

hqliving.us/binaural-beats

Here you'll find a complete article on the subject including youtube links that will direct you to two high quality binaural beats.

Binaural beats can induce different states of consciousness such as trance, relaxation or put us into an active and focused state of mind. All you need is headphones. Simply give it a try and see how you feel.

Thank you again for purchasing this book!

If you enjoyed this book, would you be kind enough to leave a review for this book on Amazon?

Thank you and good luck!

www.ingramcontent.com/pod-product-compliance
Lightning Source LLC
Chambersburg PA
CBHW071230280526
45787CB00002B/870